WHAT
ALMOST FORGOTTEN

WHAT YOU HAVE ALMOST FORGOTTEN

Selected Poems by
GYULA ILLYÉS

Edited, and with an Introduction, by
WILLIAM JAY SMITH

1999
Kortárs Kiadó, Budapest
Curbstone Press, Willimantic

FIRST EDITION, copyright © 1999 by Mária Illyés and William Jay Smith
Original poems copyright © 1928, 1930, 1935, 1937, 1938, 1939, 1940, 1942, 1946, 1947, 1949, 1950, 1956, 1961, 1963, 1965, 1968, 1973, 1974, 1977 by Mária Illyés
Introduction copyright © 1999 by William Jay Smith
Translations copyright © 1999 by Kortárs Kiadó and William Jay Smith

Certain of these translations appeared first in *The New Hungarian Quarterly*, *Translation*, and *Modern Hungarian Poetry*, edited by Miklós Vajda, New York: Columbia University Press, 1977, and Gyula Illyés, *Selected Poems*, edited by Thomas Kabdebo and Paul Tabori, London: Chatto and Windus, 1971. The Introduction, in a slightly different form, first appeared in *The Hollins Critic*, Roanoke, Virginia. The editor is grateful to these publications for permission to reprint.

This book was published with support from the National Endowment for the Arts, Connecticut Commission on the Arts, the National Cultural Fund of Hungary, and donations from many individuals.

Library of Congress Cataloging-in-Publication Data

Illyés, Gyula, 1902–1983
[Poems. English. Selections]
What you have almost forgotten: selected poems by Gyula Illyés / edited with an introduction by William Jay Smith; translated by William Jay Smith et al.–1st ed.
     p.   cm.
ISBN 1-880684-65-9 (paper)
I. Smith, William Jay, 1918–. II. Title.
PH3241.I55A276 1999
894'.511132–dc21   99-27588

CURBSTONE PRESS
321 Jackson Street Willimantic, CT 06226
e-mail: books@curbstone.org http://www.curbstone.org

Translators

John Batki
Christine Brooke-Rose
Donald Davie
Alan Dixon
Anthony Edkins
Gavin Ewart
Daniel Hoffman
Marie B. Jaffe
Thomas Kabdebo
Nicholas Kolumban
Claire Lashley
Douglas Livingstone
Kenneth McRobbie
J.G. Nichols
William Jay Smith
Charles Tomlinson
Vernon Watkins
Fred Will
John W. Wilkinson

Contents

Introduction

I

Gyula Illyés throughout his lifetime drew inspiration, like Béla Bartók in music, from Hungary's deepest roots. In his introduction to *Once Upon a Time: Forty Hungarian Folk-Tales* (1964) he says:

"The Hungarian folk-tales, clothing the peasantry's confessions in pure poetry and expressing its aspirations to a higher, freer and purer life, do more than amuse us. It was over vast distances and at the cost of untold sufferings that the Hungarians reached their country. The Hungarian folk-tale – in which the heroes embark on incredible adventures, fight with dragons, and outwit the devil – has preserved, in its fairy-like language, the ancient treasures; it has preserved an ancient Hungarian view of the world."

That ancient Hungarian view of the world is preserved not only in the folk-tales but also in the anonymous poets of the Hungarian countryside. Gyula Illyés was inspired by them both in his poetry and in his autobiographical volume *People of the Puszta*. In all his work he avoids theories and concerns himself directly and particularly with basic humanity. "For him," Jean Follain has said, "the poet remains the foremost pioneer: he alone can say at which instant man turns assassin and hangman – when originally he had been a hero. The poetry of Illyés shows us the closeness of the infinite, and of childhood, the proximity of peace and death, while it brands and denounces the tyranny bent on leading human beings astray and provoking their miserable fears and stifling the fraternity of mankind."

Gyula Illyés, who died in 1983 a few months after his eightieth birthday, was born at Rácegrespuszta in Western Hungary. His forebears had been indentured ser-

9

vants, shepherds and agricultural workmen, on a large estate; his father had risen to the position of village mechanic, and through the combined efforts of various members of his family Illyés was sent to school in the neighboring village and afterwards to high school in Budapest. He interrupted his university education to work for Red Relief, an organization that aimed to help participants in the Communist revolution of 1919. When the Communist government fell, to escape arrest, he fled in 1921 to Paris, where he lived for the next five years. While working as a bookbinder, he attended courses at the Sorbonne. He published poems in French, as well as Hungarian, and became the friend of Eluard, Crevel, Aragon, and Tzara, gaining an intimate knowledge of Dadaism and Surrealism. He could easily have stayed on in Paris and earned a reputation as a poet writing in French, but he chose to return to Hungary. This decision was the turning point in his life: he separated himself from modernist literary movements, and, inspired by the ideals of the Hungarian poet Petőfi, a brilliant biography of whom he was later to write, he set out on a conscious mission to speak for his people. On the Ile Saint-Louis in Paris, opposite the Palais Lambert, Illyés sat on a bench in 1926 to set down his poem "The Sad Field-Hand":

> The sun has hardened my crust of bread;
> Tepid is my flask
> And heavy and slow my sun-warmed blood...
>
> I remain here, irresolute, at the center of an alien field,
> A stranger for whom no one waits, and who, in the
>   autumn,
> His work completed, in the shade of a haystack,
> Will without a word sink down to join the impassive
>   earth.*

---

* Unless otherwise indicated, the translations quoted are mine, done with the assistance of Miklós Vajda and Gyula Kodolányi.

In spirit the poet had never left his native heath, and he never would.

The position of the peasantry, from which he came, was always foremost in Illyés's mind. Miklós Vajda describes visiting him some years ago: "I casually mentioned that an experimental theater company was to be formed in Budapest. He looked at me sharply, and said abruptly, 'Damn, that will cost the peasant another two eggs.' And then he broke into an impish smile. He still instinctively measures everything in terms of cost to the people, and rightly so, because this has always been a country where everything has to be done at the expense of something else; priorities are of supreme importance."

When Illyés returned from France, the poet Mihály Babits, the editor of *Nyugat (West)*, took him under his wing, and Illyés became a regular contributor to the magazine. He published several volumes of poems in the late twenties and early thirties, all dealing with the plight of the poor villagers. With the publication of his two distinguished prose works, *People of the Puszta* and *Petőfi* in 1936, he became one of the leaders of the Populist writers who sought to give expression to the feelings of the people. When *Nyugat* was closed down by the authorities and Babits died in 1941, Illyés took over as editor of *Magyar Csillag (Hungarian Star)*, and remained as its editor until the German occupation in March 1944.

Threatened with arrest, he spent most of 1944 in hiding, and completed *The Huns in Paris* (1946), a witty account of his years in Paris. In 1945 he founded a new review, *Válasz*, but when the authorities banned it because of its political pluralism in 1948, he retired and spent most of his time in his little house jutting into Lake Balaton at Tihany.

Always in the front ranks of literary movements, Illyés was even in his periods of enforced silence somehow eloquent. Because of his ability to survive and to express himself under the most difficult circumstances, some critics have spoken disparagingly of his cunning. This cunning apparently comes from an awareness of the contradictions within himself. In his youth he experienced the double family influences of Catholicism and Calvinism, and in his education he was disciplined in Gallic clarity. (The history of France, he said, is "principally characterized by striving for lucidity.") During the Stalinist period in Hungary Illyés published little, but because of his eminence as a writer the pressure on him was so great that he could not remain completely silent. He wrote at this time a poem titled "Roofers," which on the surface seems to praise people for rebuilding their houses but in realtiy is about the difficulty of writing in such a period. Illyés's most famous poem, "A Sentence for Tyranny", was written during the Stalinist era but was first published in 1956. It could not be published again in Hungary until 1989. Its concluding stanzas, brilliantly rendered into English by Vernon Watkins, demonstrate its appeal to so many people (it has been translated into more than forty languages):

> Where seek tyranny? Think again:
> Everyone is a link in the chain;
> Of tyranny's stench you are not free:
> You yourself are tyranny.
>
> Like a mole on a sunny day
> Walking in his blind, dark way,
> We walk and fidget in our rooms,
> Making a Sahara of our homes;
>
> All this because, where tyranny is
> Everything is in vain,
> Every creation, even this
> Poem I sing turns vain:
>
> Vain, because it is standing
> From the very first at your grave,
> Your own biography branding,
> And even your ashes are its slave.

Illyés received the Kossuth prize, Hungary's highest literary award, in 1948 and again in 1953. After a self-imposed silence between 1956 and 1961, the later publication of work in a wide variety of genres and the translation of selections of his poetry into several languages brought him world renown. At Knokke-le-Zoute in Belgium in 1965 he received the Grand Prix de la Biennale Internationale de Poésie. He later served as vice president of the International P.E.N. In 1972 he received the Kossuth prize for the third time, and for several years before his death was rumored to be one of the leading contenders for the Nobel Prize for Literature.

In addition to poems, essays, and biography, Illyés also produced plays. He wrote a number of historical dramas dealing with the role of ordinary men and women and the responsibility of their leaders in times of upheaval. His essay *In Charon's Barge*, on the subject of aging and death, appeared in the late sixties. His poetry, which became more and more contemplative towards the end of his life, lost nothing of its incisiveness.

In *People of the Puszta* (1936) Illyés tells of growing up with the people of his village, whose lives in many ways resembled those of the serfs in feudal times. As an attentive and compassionate witness in this book, Illyés is able to document exactly what life was like for him, and what it had been like for his parents and grandparents, on the *puszta* that he knew as a child. When it was first published, Illyés's fellow poet Babits read the book as if it were a travelogue "about a so-far undiscovered continent and its natives" and as if he were part of an expedition exploring it, all the more sensational because this undiscovered continent happened to be a corner of the country, of his birth and because conventionally the *puszta* of the book's title, the unlimited expanse of the Hungarian plains, existed in the Hungarian and indeed in the European imagination as an "idyllic land of freedom." The *puszta* that Illyés describes, in alarming contrast, was still in the first third of the twentieth century a place where workmen lived in wretched overcrowded conditions, working an eighteen-hour day, and starving "quietly and regularly." The book shocked his own countrymen and it continues to shock the world. In New Zealand schools it became compulsory reading for its revelation of the enduring nature of European feudalism.

Interwoven with the precise documentation, in a kind of contrapuntal fashion, is the precise memory of how everything appeared to a sensitive young boy who was destined to become a great poet. This double, and powerfully ironic, vision gives this book its unique quality. "One feels throughout," Louis Guilloux has said, "that the author, born a peasant himself, has remained one in his way of seeing and knowing, and in his way of expressing himself, that he has inherited some of the basic universal qualities of peasants anywhere, which are prudence, exactitude of judgment, and honesty when it comes to explaining things or in predicting what the weather will be like. Before it is good or bad, a thing is either true or false. Gyula Illyés never cheats; one does not cheat with evidence. If one presents oneself as a witness, one does not cheat either with oneself; one pays attention. The art of Gyula Illyés indeed at every moment is proof that he does."

In 1962 Illyés published a sequel to *People of the Puszta*, *Luncheon at the Mansion*, and in 1979 another remarkable autobiographical work, *Beatrice's Pages*. If he had written no poetry but only these prose works, he would still be deserving of attention as an important writer. In *Luncheon at the Mansion* Illyés's double and masterfully ironic vision is again present in a lighter but none the less probing vein. Here the worldly peasant-poet returns after World War II to meet face to face the fallen aristocrat, whom he had known as a child. In the moving and hilarious opening scene of the book, the poet enters the big house that he was never able to enter as a boy. And it is significant and supremely ironic that he enters it through the back door. (The back door is now the front door of the Count's reduced lodgings.) He confronts not only his father's former master but, in the person of the Count's grandson who is playing with the same toys that he once had, he contemplates the boy that he was.

Beatrice's Pages is further proof of Illyés's ability to bear witness in a profound and moving way. The book deals with the year 1919 when Illyés, at the age of seventeen, fresh from his native *puszta*, became involved in Budapest with the working-class revolution and the short-lived Republic of Councils. He worked for the illegal organization known as Red Relief, which distributed funds among those who had supported the republic. With a cheap paperback edition of *Paradise Lost* in his pocket, the young poet finds his way into the clean, well-kept kitchen of a workman's daughter. In describing the effect of this visit on him, Illyés produced pages that deserve a place beside the greatest autobiographical and confessional writings of the twentieth century.

II

In both his poetry and his prose Gyula Illyés might be termed a lyric realist. Edwin Morgan has called him one who like Robert Burns "gave the land a voice." In 1928 he wrote:

What you have almost forgotten –
The speech of your quiet people – learn again!
More reviving than a glass of fresh water
Is their hearty welcome to the tired traveller,
A welcome that brims with friendly warmth.
See how here among the villagers waiting to be paid
You too nod agreement when they speak, as they
Tell of their destiny in their own rough words,
Give reasons for their poverty.
Eager life flutters birdlike
In the difficult movements of their lips.

(translated by Gavin Ewart)

If, as some critics have found, his poetry at times appears to be lacking in mystery, it may be that he tries too strongly to adopt the speech of his "quiet people," to speak directly, and to disguise nothing.

What is immediately striking in the poetry of Illyés is its immense variety. He makes use of every kind of stanza form and every line length; he is equally at home in very formal stanzas and in impressionistic prose poems. In the couplets of "Aboard the Santa Maria" the poet, on his misty ledge overlooking Lake Balaton at Tihany, pictures himself as Columbus aboard the Santa Maria:

> Buttressed forth, a hanging garden there,
> the terrace like a ship divides the air.
>
> A table of stone, a rickety chicken coop
> emerge through holes within the shifting fog...
>
> And now when the pounding waves reach up to me,
> I feel I am centuries ago at sea...

Always in his poetry, as in *People of the Puszta*, he has an eye for precise, concrete detail. That detail can be exquisite and delicate as in "The Approaching Silence:"

> Lightly clad, on tiptoe, the little rain has just run into the garden through the gate. Is the sunlight here? The rain stops, listens, gazing at itself in the glass balls, shifts its weight; draws away. But it is still here; now and then its drops continue to fall.

or in the Mozartian final stanzas of "A World in Crystal:"

> Now furtively I stroll
>   among the cherry trees
> with their Japanese red tea
>   service of porcelain.
> All detachable beauty

causes me pain. I live
in fear for all the fragile
values of this earth.

or terrifying, as in "While the Record Plays:"

They heated hatchet blades over gas fires in roadside
workshops and hammered them into cleavers.

They brought wooden blocks on trucks and carried
them across these new provinces grimly, quickly,
and steadily: almost according to ritual.

Because at any time – at noon or midnight – they would
arrive at one of these impure settlements,

where women did not cook nor make beds as theirs
did, where men did not greet one another as they
did, where children and the whole damned com-
pany did not pronounce words as they did, and
where the girls kept apart from them.

They would select from these insolent and intolerable
people twelve men, preferably young ones, to take
to the marketplace,

and there – because of *blah-blah-blah* and moreover
quack-quack-quack and likewise *quack-blah-quack*
– would beat and behead them,

of historical necessity – because of *twaddle-twiddle* and
twiddle-diddle, and expertly, for their occupations
would be different one from the other...

Although he was able as a boy to take the killing of pigs
and chickens on the *puszta* in stride, he tells us in
"Work", his first "really shattering experience" came
when watching the hooping of a cartwheel. The lesson
of the craftsmen he witnessed he retained for a lifetime:

The wood caught fire; they poured a bucket of water on it. The wheel sent up steam and smoke so thick you couldn't see it. But still the hammer pounded on, and still came the "Press hard"! uttered breathlessly from the corner of the mouth. The fire blazed up again. Water flung again as on a tortured man who has sunk into a coma. Then the last flourishing bush of steam evaporated while the apprentices poured a thin trickle from a can on the cooling iron which, in congealing, gripped lovingly its life-long companion to be. The men wiped the sweat from their brows, spat, shook their heads, satisfied. Nothing – not the slightest flicker of a movement – could have been executed differently.

Like his father and his grandfather before him, Illyés had a deep respect for his craft. At the end of many of his poems one can almost sense the poet, like his peasant forebears, wiping the sweat from his brow, satisfied with the artifact that he has created, for which nothing "could have been executed differently."

This sense of craft is carried to a point of extreme sophistication and subtlety in "The Maker," which might have come from the pen of Paul Valéry:

> More ardent
> than two lithe bodies dancing
> together, embracing
> those two
> thoughts so different from each other
> frolicked and turned
> struggling
> for life, for death,
> finding their fulfilment
> in a third.
> *(translated by Daniel Hoffman)*

For all the autobiographical detail in Illyés's poems, he always maintains a classical distance. Not long before his death Illyés was asked about these lines which he wrote in 1934:

MASK

Whatever I say, it covers, it conceals,
Like a mask dangles between you and me.
I smile, while, with its distorted grimaces,
Whatever I don't speak about, pants like a murderer,
Bares its teeth, rattles, wants just blood, just pain.
I wait with irony for the moment when you will
shoot me in the head.

(translated by Miklós Vajda)

To what extent, he was asked, could this poem be taken seriously and if there were for him such a thing as a mask, what indeed did it conceal. Illyés's answer (the poem was one that he disliked and dropped from his later collections) tells a great deal about the nature of his poetry: "This is a many-layered thing. There are indeed poets who like to display themselves. I have already said that trying to please in art, which with some doesn't always stop short of mincing, is far from rare. That's why there are poets whose private lives are more successful works than those they have actually written... I was brought up on the *puszta* in a smallish family circle and I can still remember my father's words, his parting advice, when I went away to secondary school. He said: 'And I don't want to hear anything about you!' This is not really hiding... This is what a man should be – modest. Even young girls can be immodest but it is unbecoming in a man. For me, it is something of a contradiction that a man can be an artist: that he conceives, that he goes into labor, that he gives birth... I've never been able to be happy with this coincidence of usage in the language. Serious creators, Michelangelo and his like, have never gone in for this kind of thing. It's none of the audience's business to know how someone works. It really is difficult to create something which is good."

19

Even when speaking of social injustice, as he does eloquently in one of his finest poems, "Wonder Castle," he maintains a certain reserve. In this poem, written in 1937, he tells of arriving in Budapest from the country and of taking the funicular up the Buda hills to the more affluent section of the city:

It was as if, from the hell of the plain below us,
we were borne up from circle to circle
into some present-day Turkish heaven.
Or, with the old look-out tower
it was like a magic castle,
the terrifying or happy
seat of some Asiatic deity
found only in Hungarian and Vogul folk-tale,
called Castle Spinning on a Duck's Leg: Wonder Castle.

(translated by Kenneth McRobbie)

But he finds little wonder on the faces of the high-society figures he encounters in this wonder castle. He examines them closely and records their true lineaments with savage satire. At the end of the poem he has a vision of the plain from which he has come rising up, as it does in the folk-tale, and bringing down the towers on the hill. But even if such a revolution were to occur, the poet affirms that he would still want to retain his objective posture as a dispassionate observer.

In his introduction to the anthology *Modern Hungarian Poetry*, Miklós Vajda points out that poetry in Hungary has had through the centuries a special position never equalled by the other arts: "Poetry, which cannot be shelled like a city, or whitewashed like murals, crushed like sculpture, closed like theaters, or even banned and censored as easily as novels and journals, can spread and be influential even without print or manuscript. And so it dominated the literature of a people that had to live under difficult conditions, luring the best talents and forc-

20

ing them to lead dangerous lives and produce extraordinary achievements." Gyula Illyés was the living embodiment of this poetic tradition. In one of his later poems, "A Wreath," he pays tribute to the Hungarian language, which is spoken by no more than fifteen million people, a third of whom live outside the country. The poem is a passionate statement addressed to his mother tongue, evoking those who have struggled to keep it alive:

You can no longer
soar. And yet you blaze,
wind-slit Hungarian tongue, sending
your snakelike flames along the ground, hissing
at times with pain,
more often with the helpless rage of the humiliated,
your guardian angels forsaking you...
language of the Kassa black marketeer, the
Bucharest servant girl,
the Beirut whore, all calling
for mother, behold your son, spittle
on his rage-reddened face,
master of many tongues,
held worthy of attention by other nations
for what, as a loyal European,
he has to say:
he cannot mount any festive platform,
cannot accept any wreath,
however glorious, which he would not, stepping
        quickly down,
carry over to lay at your feet, and with his smile
        draw forth
on your agonizing lips,
your smile, my beloved, ever-nurturing mother.

The reference to the Bucharest servant girl reminds us that in the last decade of his life Illyés spoke out in a series of articles against what he called the cultural genocide of more than two million Hungarians residing in Transylvania. He had treated the subject years before, in its full brutality, in "While the Record Plays." Illyés was not an apologist for socialism nor a public defender of any system or theory. He continued, a literary giant, throughout his life to attack injustice wherever he found it, and to promote passionately, and with the power and balance of his art, a civilized view of humanity.

The translators of the poems in this volume have worked under a severe handicap: almost all of them know little or no Hungarian; they have worked with Miklós Vajda, Illyés's son-in-law Gyula Kodolányi, and other informants who have provided them with precise literal versions of the poems. And yet while thus handicapped, they have had one great advantage. Most of them are poets in their own right and have done everything possible, going in some instances to great extremes to approximate the poetic form of the original, to produce translations that qualify as poems in English. These translations have been done over a period of more than thirty years; a number of them first appeared in *A Tribute to Gyula Illyés*, edited by Thomas Kabdebo and Paul Tabori, with a Preface by Jean Follain, published in 1968 by Occidental Press, Washington, D.C. and reprinted in Gyula Illyés, *Selected Poems*, edited by Thomas Kabdebo and Paul Tabori, published in 1971 by Chatto and Windus, London. I am grateful to Mr. Kabdebo and to the late Mr. Tabori for their pioneering work without which this enlarged selection would not have been possible, and for Mr. Kabdebo's permission to reprint these translations, which in the latter volume, had the further advantage of having been vetted by the poet C. Day Lewis.

William Jay Smith

Books Mentioned in the Introduction

ONCE UPON A TIME:
FORTY HUNGARIAN FOLK-TALES.
English translation, Barna Balogh, Susan Kun, Ruth Sutter. Budapest:
Corvina Press, 1964.

PEOPLE OF THE PUSZTA.
English translation, G. F. Cushing. Budapest: Corvina Press, 1967.
London: Chatto and Windus. 1973.

A TRIBUTE TO GYULA ILLYÉS.
Thomas Kabdebo and Paul Tabori (editors), Preface by Jean Follain.
Washington: Occidental Press, 1968.

CEUX DES PUSZTAS.
French translation by Véronique Charaire, Preface by Louis Guilloux.
Paris: Gallimard, 1969.

SELECTED POEMS.
Thomas Kabdebo and Paul Tabori (editors). Foreword by Thomas
Kabdebo. London: Chatto and Windus, 1971.

PETŐFI
English translation, G. F. Cushing. Budapest: Corvina Press, 1973.

MODERN HUNGARIAN POETRY.
Miklós Vajda (editor). New York: Columbia University Press, 1977.

Essays, poems, and interviews appeared
in the NEW HUNGARIAN QUARTERLY.

What You Have Almost Forgotten

What you have almost forgotten –
The speech of your quiet people – learn again!
More reviving than a glass of fresh water
Is their hearty welcome to the tired traveller,
A welcome that brims with friendly warmth.

See how here among the villagers waiting to be paid
You too nod agreement when they speak, as they
Tell of their destiny in their own rough words,
Give reasons for their poverty.
Eager life flutters birdlike
In the difficult movements of their lips.

In Kaposvár, in a young street which has no name yet,
On All Souls' Night a man asked me for a light –
        the wind
Blew as we huddled together, our coats over us,
As if embracing.
I looked into his face in the matchlight.
He smiled at me.
Our hearts recognised each other for a moment.

Another day I sat in a pub and a thin tailor
Asked to sit beside me, with such gusto as if
He were unpacking his good home-made lunch for me
        to share.
He unpacked his life before me
(The previous week a daughter had been born).

As the faces open to you, shine at you, your own
        face clears
And shines more warmly in the warmth of theirs.
Don't be ashamed
That you feel your grandmother's eyes

Are what you see with,
That your heart simmered like a happy samovar;
    it boiled
When you told good news to an old driver,
You felt the hot steam in your face
And stuttered of happiness.

On this dry, rough, rocky ground
The roots of your moods find the sweet earth
Through small crevices.
The openings are a happy smile,
The pupil of an eye that widened.

This soil will feed you. So that your song is like
The rustling of deep-rooted oak trees,
Like the heartbeats of the topmost leaves,
As they chatter, telling secrets
Of distant winds.

[1928]   (Gavin Ewart)

The Sad Field-Hand

The sun has hardened my crust of bread;
Tepid is my flask
And heavy and slow my sun-warmed blood.
Seated amid the steam of my worry and my sweat,
I watch the silent fields pitch around me.
It is noon.
Deep in the woods the wind and the future repose.

The overseer passes in his carriage.
My weary hand lifts my hat;
I am covered with ash and grime,
The gaze of my cattle refreshes my heart.

Beyond the dust, beyond the trees,
Beyond the spread of clouds, the fronded dust,
There where the indifferent sun reels on its way
Lie distant cities with illuminated squares wheeling
        beneath the stars,
And seas, floating islands, and flaming mountains of
        gold,
Of all these I have heard –
Of heaven and earth bursting with riches,
        and yet
I remain here, irresolute, at the center of an alien field,
A stranger for whom no one waits, and who, in the
        autumn,
His work completed, in the shade of a haystack,
Will without a word sink down to join the impassive
        earth.

[1928]   (William Jay Smith)

27

At the Turning Point of Life

Night envelops us: clouds rest, darkness drizzles –
outside, the branches are bare and glittering wet;
as the wind sweeps by, they let fall their tears –
youth is passing.

Before my window two swallows dive, dip down,
almost hand in hand like fish at the bottom of the sea.
One is love, I thought, and the other, secret hope.
All that accompanied me flees, quietly retreating to a
    truer homeland.

And now in her loose robes, with large, disproportionate
limbs, monster Melancholy sits down beside me,
drawing my head to her moist breast,
and mocks me: Weep if you dare, weep, unhappy one...

Mourn if you have anything to mourn for! Examine
    your life:
Around you autumn rain pours down and mist covers
    the wooded hills;
frothy, filthy water rushes toward you down the
    sloping road
where once with sinister intent you led your beloved.

Like prayer beads, drops run down the windowpane.
O you nimble minutes, seasons, centuries! – Autumn
    twilight covers the paper
over which I lean as to a mirror, twilight that soon will
    cover my young face.
Through trickling drops I watch the brown trees swing,
    reaching into the mist.

[1930]   (William Jay Smith)

28

The Defeated Army

That's what we need that fat barmaid and those
    carousing wild men.
Pots smashed against the wall... and that tablecloth
    spotted with red wine like a winter battlefield.
Wine, smoke, a poorly lit room, that's what we need
    from now on, that and a dirty male song.
The noise of the coins that grimy hands hurl at them

and the thick laughter of the waitresses with their
    insolent replies.
Shout, good fellow! and roar if you wish to drown out
    the sorrowful cry of your soul and the frightful
    noise of the victory that cracks and crumbles...
    You who once placed your head
on a virgin's breast, listening to her anxious heartbeats,

lean now over that smelly girl.
You can laugh and thrust her into a corner.
If it's time for the tumble, well, go to it, your shame
    and your self both flung
far away from your future, driven from your high
    hopes. Hide your face that burns in those filthy
    arms
and may you be dragged down to the true depth of
    your destiny.
The fine army has fled. Drunk with blood, with war
    cries, the dead remain on the ground, and the
    enemy, shouting, carts away their bodies
in his great convoys... The man who flees, the
    coward, runs through an ash-strewn night as if
    through his life, and licks his sweat.
He couldn't die; he continues to wander, his shadow
    hungry.
He runs below the window, skids on the ice, swears,

sits on the ground,
comes to drink with the others, sinks down... Around
    him hover the fresh landscapes of old.
He watches, begins to weep, leans on someone's
    shoulder.

Outside, the wind continues to rant. Shut up, old
    show-off, spirit of our fathers!
Freedom, sacred vengeance?... A puff of breath and
    the lamp flickers, and sputtering chokes
and dies. It stinks. Now Tragedy comes on. And you,
    noble Music, call forth the cries of the girls, the
    thick laughter, the curses, the pounding on the
    table... The bottle

leaps up, falls, and spits blood. The man without hope
    has also died.
Bad memories, my lasting friends, the dance is yours!
    Drop by drop puss streaks down the windows...
    Far behind, moving slowly as in nightmare
across our beaten earth, upright in his stirrups,
the Conqueror with the voice of a horse gazes around
    him through the falling snow on a deserted
    landscape.

[1930]   *(William Jay Smith)*

30

Siblings

For three days, I would have only gazed
at the shaded valley of your eyes, your eyebrows,
        raised
above thick reeves of your lashes among which
tiny pools of lively waters itch
flashing their light, their agile schemes
the frolicking of little slippery breams.
For three days, as if on silence hooked,
into the one then into the other I'd have looked.

And another three days I would have spent
watching silently only the soft bend
of what is barely a hint under your dress,
and the little stars which slumber on your breasts
and prepare, arching the spokes of light,
to dazzle in the darkness of the night.
For three days, as if on silence hooked,
into the one then into the other I'd have looked.

And again, it would have been enough for me,
to graze my eyes on you, to watch you silently,
your twin knees, to a lovely stem growing,
and shyly challenging each other, drawing
like the double wings of a gate apart,
each other they might have encouraged: to part.
For three days, as if on silence hooked,
into the one then into the other I'd have looked.

In the mellow heat which gently poured
from your shining body I would soon have cured
myself, bathing in your light which shone,
on me, as on a sick man shines the sun,
watching stealthily, how in my chest
pain prickles and dissolves, and how the rest

of the body would itself dissolve into the sky
of an airier landscape, into a lullaby.

And I would have been a child, your child,
so that if I hug you, I'd hug you like a child,
that your tender voice could then be heard,
to get from you now the consoling word.
I hugged you so, brother his sister twin
the taste of ancient lust lessening the sin:
your most faithful lover, I was asleep fast,
by the time the first night, spent together, passed.

[1930]   *(Thomas Kabdebo)*

Bandit

His brows, like tousled bushes caught
in snow, the droop of his moustache,
while in the crevice of each ear
sprouted another snowy bush.
What hair he had upon his head –
retreating, hoary hair – was blown
like frosty sky swept by the wind
whirling above a wintry scene.
That I recall, and how his eye,
one good eye, like a winter sun
appearing, disappearing in
a frozen puddle, shyly shone.
His voice, too, like the winter wind,
or like that anguish hoarsely howled
by packs of wolves who far away,
and even now, are being killed.
He stood framed by the door. He wolfed
away at the huge mug of soup,
and with a somewhat shaky hand
wiped from his chin and chest each drop.
Then, humbly setting down the mug
before our gentle mother, he
wished us 'God bless', and stumbled off
towards the hill uncertainly.
He went, a fragment of a white
and winter's tale, hesitantly.
He went as he had come, upon
that close, oppressive summer's day.

[1935]   *(J. G. Nichols)*

The Apricot-Tree

I

The apricot-tree
shoulder-high or less –
Look! an apricot
at branch-tip ripeness.

Stretching, straining,
holding out a prize,
the tree is a maiden
offering closed eyes.

You stand and wonder:
will she bend and sway
her slender waist or
step back, run away.

With quick breath shudders
from heat or passion,
fans herself, signals
in the high fashion.

Shakes the shimmering
pomp out of her dress,
then blushing she waits
for your compliments.

This garden a ballroom,
she gazes about,
anxiously, constantly,
wants to be sought out.

II

I spend each evening
all evening with her.
Come again tomorrow
she says in whisper.

She rustles softly
when I salute her.
It seems my poetry
can still transmute her.

Sweet apricot-tree,
in a dream I saw
the cool arbour, and you
on the crackling straw.

First you glanced around
anxiously, then left
the dark hedge, the well,
in your moon-white shift.

Your stepping increased
the silence gently,
brought me your body
soft and sweet-scented.

Since that dream I glance
towards you, flushing.
Please look at me too,
askance and blushing.

[1937]
   (Christine Brooke-Rose)

You Cannot Escape

We looked down into the ship's engine-room
where, among the pistons' steady beat
naked stokers scurried about
crimson as devils in the heat;
great gusts of boiling air escaped
the hatch as if from a door in hell –
What toil! I thought... but someone beside me
said: They're used to it, they know it well.

Sitting in a deckchair by the rail,
upon my lap a folded book,
blue mountains swam alongside, past me,
soothing my eyes, absorbing my tired look.
Hills and clouds of water – an unwritten
poem was all this, too – the slow
voyage – images woven in rhythms
to the muffled thumping below.

I swam over water, soared with the light,
happily knew I was beyond all now
high on the world's poetic stratum,
leaving below the unceasing row
of sweating and spitting and choking.
They're used to it, I told myself at last.
Or are they? And arrowing into me
came a cold sardonic shaft from the past.

Oh, are they? Did *you* ever get used to
(– you had a share in it –) that hoe?
Do you remember? Recall your father!
What did he get used to? His final blow?
In the midst of fate and poverty
what man can get used to anything?
Agonised, I paced up and down
on a ship's deck, feeling its writhing.

You are a fool, I told myself.
A traitor! just a traitor, nothing more,
amplified a voice in my heart,
while the moving deck groaned to its core:
Traitor! Liar! Miserable one!
Hireling, lying low! If once again
you found yourself among life's stokers
would you get used to the choking and pain?

I found myself against the rail
struggling, as if my father's fate
were cast beneath my feet, as if he stoked
again, day-labourer on the count's estate.
As if my father and all my ancestors
were toiling, panting, choking down below
and crying upwards from the grave –
the deck made knuckles rap against my sole.

Staring down at the water I saw
the blue landscape loping fast
away as if the motion weren't the ship's
but a panting history rushing past.
As if it flung at me its ragings,
sickening me, its pitiless No
 – spelling it out – you cannot forget,
you cannot escape, wherever you go.

[1937]   *(Douglas Livingstone)*

The Wonder Castle

I'd arrived the previous night from the country.
Next morning, my eyes were casting about anxiously
for (like an old coat
the body feels easy in) the run-down countryside
where I'd lately been on a four-week visit,
so familiar and roomy, floating in sunshine,
where I feel at home, where in the rag-fluttering dust
man and beast lick parched lips;
but enough said
on that subject
– why go on about my home in the country?

In a word, I'd only been back in Budapest
a day, still feeling a trifle
awkward like one just
come up to town on his first trip
– a little awed, not yet used
to the everywhere apparent more-of-everything.
I wore it uneasily like a newly starched shirt
next to the skin, when
I had to go out visiting
– or, let's say, up the Rácz Hill on an excursion.

Then home and its memories
would buzz in my ears, get in my eyes,
so that I felt I was climbing
up the Hill straight from the puszta's
evening fields, where many times
I'd written out day-laborers' schedules.

I'll tell you why I thought that way,
looking at the ticket in my hand
in my seat on the Cog-wheel Railway:
for should a peasant have a mind
to take the self-same ride,
he'd dig for his ticket an entire working day.
At home seventy fillers is a whole day's pay.

There we were, some hundred or more
in comfort, legs crossed, for the full
price of a vineyard worker's labor
gliding up the back of the Hill.

A villa, a flower garden
floated past; on a sand-strewn
flat roof two young women taking sun;
further off in the shade of a walnut
someone dealt cards on a green table;
somewhere a radio was humming.
The higher we got
the cooler the air, the less dust;
faces were a carefully even tan.
It was as if, from the hell of the plain below us,
we were borne up from circle to circle
into some present-day Turkish heaven.
Or, with the old look-out tower
it was like a magic castle,
the terrifying or happy
seat of some Asiatic deity
found only in Hungarian and Vogul folk-tale,
called Castle Spinning on a Duck's Leg: Wonder Castle.

Over a hedge flew tennis balls
and as though in competition after
them, like invisible flights of birds,
balls of happy girlish laughter,
laughter that rose the higher.

– And this no weekend, but a working day.
The afternoon was half-way to summer sunset
in a blue sky with faint silver streaked,
heat glowed only in the green light
of the tree-tops' dying lamp, smokily.
It was a weekday, but suffused with peace
and brimming with luminous grace
such as no religion ever gave in a week of Sundays.
Across lamplit leaves
to faint music, where trees afforded shelter,
glimmering like a dream
a knot of girls circled, pirouetted, weaving
the spell of an unattainable, tender future
over the hearts of rapacious nomads,
like Dul's daughters once in Meotian marshes.

Paper lanterns flashed on in a plane-tree
setting another scene – a gent in pyjamas,
somewhat paunchy, leaning back with cigar
in the wine-tinged light – a figure
reclining in the ease of Property
like some cartoon for the Communist Party.
By then the whole Hill
sparkled with lights, and still
it rose every minute higher.
I alone recalled the landscape's flat table
far below, perhaps now underground even, the people,
the country
which just might have heard some story
about it, yet
like a blind plodding horse still drives the mill
– this modish sleek curvature,
this real live Eden of a Hill
where electricity flames more lavishly,
for instance, than in all of Tolna County.

I looked about me. A hill further
off lit up, and then another
like brother beacons.
Soon, will-o'-the-wisp-like hundreds beckon
shrieking, dancing; they all spun
around upon swamps of blindest misery
in each of the universe's regions.

Very beautiful, I thought; but I am too tired
to join the choir
providing this glittering merry-go-round's music.

The outdoor restaurant's
seventy or more tables of idly chattering
diners will consume at one sitting
as much as, even at a rough count
– such were my thoughts, grinding underfoot
the stubbornly unyielding material, as in my poetry
I'd always grappled with raw reality
in the hope that someday it would fuse and shine.
Supper here would cost a week's wages
I reckoned, expertly; almost enthusiastically
I pictured to myself the pumps,
delicate piping, capillaries
sucking all this up, for there's no surplus,
well-kneaded, boiled,
mashed, several times cooled,
over from those
who swallow their spittle at home with us.

Outside the garden – where daily
a crunched bridge and hospital
melt on the tongues of this charmingly
cavorting throng, along with the future of thirty thousand
stillborn infants –
a parade was on: the milling casual
lookers-on applauded, laughed.

In the moon-shading bushes
were silent couples making love on benches,
dreamily (spooningly, I'm inclined to call it)
in pastry-shops others chatted,
and whatever cares they had
were triple-distilled,
delicate as angels' wings.

Oh poet! Be on the look-out
for wonder, for the unusual
that delights the eye and heart
just because someone points a finger at it:
a swineherd among this happy lot, for example,
a reaper, a shepherd
nonchalantly sipping iced pineapple
in a reclining chair, or leisurely
picking broken straw from between his toes
– some new color, some new face amid this uniformity
that for a millennium has bored us, heaven knows!
A potter, a miner, a baker
who, I'm sure, would like to see just what
his creations are up to out in the world, like a mother
wonders about her children who are far from her
– but I saw not one of those I sought.

The monotonous crowd reclined, stretched, ambled;
like moon-blazed foreheads in a herd of horses
here and there went revered personages
well-known to all,
as among us the count, the priest and judge.

And others hard at their heels:
with such dignified mien newspaper hacks,
squeamish mass-circulation tycoons
who pay hard-working loyal goons
to do their blackmail behind their backs.

With a girl on each arm, an employment
agency boss erect, with smiling face
strutted with a paper in his pocket
certifying he was a mental case.

There, with face pensive and woebegone
lifted towards the moon
(as if to take a swig from it)
having polished off a large chicken,
sat the celebrated playwright;
you'd swear that in no time at all
he might say something original.

Under a sunshade (much like a market woman's)
a very proper gentleman, noted for this,
was offering his wife for sale
– discreetly covered with a veil –
we nibbled at her apricot smile
as if we'd been offered a bowl of fruit.
However, no one fancied the deal.
And... why go on? The faces were so alike,
as I've said, that being unable to tell them apart
is quite disturbing for a lover of art.

As they talked, marriageable maidens
fluttered the whitest of hands
whose long nails seemed to indicate
that they had never cleaned a grate.
So I took a good look
at God's chosen ones, these fairy folk
in suits and shirts of silk
that permitted glimpses of hairy arms and chests,
and meekly
– with heart so long barred from feeling passionately,
only humbly, and with a servant's wisdom –
for my spirit was above
envy or incitement;
mine was a reputation for being peaceable, quiet
and so patient that I blush for it

(I do not judge, I merely watch, the world)

not to mention being rich,
or regarded as such
with regular meals and a bed to sleep in.

Well – like a scout surveying new territory
lately emerged from archetypal slime,
during that glistening evening
I was thinking about just this one thing
as I looked about me, quietly:

Once the marsh rises
– were it ever to rise – to topple
the myriad towers and huge axle
of this glittering miracle
all coming to pass as in the old tale,
that "grass grow not, nor stone remain on stone"

I would even then
stand aside, still play the quiet man,
so that when all came tumbling down
order might be kept,
and calmly, impartially, I should
be able to give account
of how life was before the flood
in this pre-historic period.

[1937]   *(Kenneth McRobbie)*

44

Fatherland in the Heights

A time may come when to remember
Shall ask more courage than to plan,
To claim the past more than the future
In seeking a new fatherland.

What do I care? My land already
Holds, more than any height, all steady.
I walk, look around, live, nothing else:
I have found a weapon, magic spells.

I already share it, too, if I come
To tell you its nature, this secret home.
Murmur a line of Petőfi, friend:
In a magic circle at once you stand.

If this pure land's overrun by invaders,
A new Tartar horde or a horde of traders,
If our paths are twisted and made to squirm,
Just as when somebody treads on a worm,

Then speak to yourself, with eyes closed,
Just speak those words which at one time caused
Sands drifting, peoples, houses
To compose the pattern Hungary rouses.

Enraged rivers learnt gentleness,
Or defiant cliffs – do not forget this,
If we go back, proud-lipped, unsacred,
Into our fortresses, our secrets.

For mere chilling horror cannot chill us,
The merely murderous cannot kill us;
Weave your bullet-proof vest of language right,
Declaim our Berzsenyi into the night.

Gather friend, all you learnt to see
When you walked in meadows which then were free,
All the spoil of the heart's and the mind's dominions,
In gay disputes, with girls for companions.

As Noah into the Ark brought kinds,
Bring every example of thought, the mind's,
The number of yearnings, orphaned, tell,
And your dreams' menagerie, as well.

Though for a thousand years to come,
Like an echo unchallenged, they lie quite dumb,
Your words shall answer the questioners' wonder
Then with the more surprising thunder.

Watch, then, and take the lesson to heart
Which is mute, though it reaches places apart:
Clasping my book in close embrace,
I look and laugh in my enemy's face.

For if I stand nowhere, I still can be
At home, at the heart of what I see,
Even if there my world is shown
Like a *fata morgana*, upside down.

So I remain a messenger here
With the precious graveyards in my care.
If the order to shoot me through the forehead is given,
Whatever there rests, escapes into heaven.

[1939]   *(Vernon Watkins)*

Face Down

Face down in the mud, as if grenades
    were disputing above,
I throw myself down, flatten out, shout
    in this blind love.

I would crouch beside you – but aren't you
    the enemy I must fight?
Would you accept me as a friend if I were
    driven against you in the night?

I whisper the password, the ancient one! – how often
    I've whispered it in vain!
I love you, will you love me even after you have
    fallen into my arms, when slain?

Is it not simply shelter I want? Peace, even the peace
    of quick death which then
is opened by love – until the bomb-flame of the sun
    shines on us again?

Oh, sad peace. No enemy, no friend: only
    as on a field of war
arms and legs stiffened in their last convulsions,
    embracing the air.

I quietly ready myself – oh, sad
    sinister resurrection –
like the soul taken to his lord by an angel
    only for rejection.

[1937]   (Fred Will)

47

Rivers, Fjords, Small Villages...

Waterloo, Wagram, Mohi – what were they
Before their mild and empty names were filled
With keenings, and a thousand deaths went sailing
Away to shell the overcast? Unskilled
We were in you, in fjord, hamlet, field
And equable river. And your fate incurred
Ought to have been, and ought to be today,
      To persevere unheard.

But thus the earth expands. New meadowlands,
New mountains in the mind of the child at school
Rise where gun barrels probe the map and point
To what they meant, being devastation's fool,
To erase from earth. The gun's a new ferrule
For the geography master, bright and burning
Milestone on the one old road that bends
      Towards one more turning.

One more, mankind? I who walked trusting by
Your side, now stand apart. Or do I plead
Against the tide, standing upon some whirled
Shipboard? If sin on sin is all the seed
Your learning sows, why then, my kind, indeed
Your servitude of spirit has to be
(An envious god's curse) endless. I shall cry
      As long as I can, my plea.

Be mute, Petsamo, bay and virgin hill
And you, secluded vales and homesteads; hounds
Couched to await a carcass like Sedan!
And you, small isles where Death the discoverer
      grounds
His keel, and an undreamed-of epoch founds!

Small places, new Americas, so long
Doomed to great fame, whose ruinous bounties
   swell,
      Be mute – nay, howl! Give tongue!

And see your destiny through. Come brighten, burn
And so many new stars! Ranked in armies, make
Not only history to a new design
But a new geometry on a sky in wreck.
And you, Petsamo, lurid bloody speck,
Rise, a new dispensation, on our sight:
That some time Man: in time to come, shall turn
      More hopefully, to the height...

[1943, published 1947]   *(Donald Davie)*

Sacrifice

The lines I fashioned yesterday,
I have destroyed completely;
Lest they be found and I confess,
I will disown them neatly.
Today another thought arose,
An image longs to greet us;
But I am strangling this one too –
This living poem-foetus.
Still kicking, sense stirs inside you?
To life do you feel driven?
Are you a poem? Would you speak?
Then shout, corpse, up to heaven.

[1944, published 1945]

(Marie B. Jaffe)

Horror

I saw: Budapest burning:
around a people's head
before its fall, a glowing
wreath of fire; war; war dead.

I saw – as if someone else –
amid wild briarbush
of exploding shell, a corpse,
a nightmare carcass, crushed.

There was moonlight that morning,
six o'clock, New Year's day;
the housewreck I was standing
on, at dawn, turned grey.

Like Moses' bushes, burning,
each shell, with rapid shriek,
burst, screaming something –
God or Fate tried to speak.

In the icy snow of the street
I saw a human head,
a bas-relief trampled flat
by some inhuman tread.

I saw a baby, still blind,
close to its dead mother:
not milk to suck but blood,
blood not wool for cover.

The baby raised its bloody face
and cried out to the dead.
His mother was – , this very place;
himself – the years ahead.

[1945]   *(Anthony Edkins)*

At Plovdiv

Plovdiv, the Philippopolis of the ancients.
There too the Hotel Lamartine detained us
(It's that vast Greek-style place – no less would do
for the poet with his sixty horses and his retinue,
he talks of it at length, if I'm not wrong,
in his 'Voyage en Orient').
'Here is the room', said Peter, his tone heartfelt,
'where the great genius dwelt!'
'To tell the truth, it's overhead,' amended
the stockingless young matron, 'but the corn is spread
to dry up there, so nowadays it's our own
room that we show to the visitors, it must be said
this one's a good deal nicer.' And she showed us
the pieces put by for her daughter's bottom drawer
and all the family photos, an entire army
of spruced-up sons- and daughters-in-law, with a speech
on the mode of existence, past and present, of each.
She pointed out, among so many more
the poet too. 'We brought him down a floor,
mice swarm up there. And he's not out of place
here, poor thing – not a bad-looking face
his, either.' And she dusted off the likeness,
even as she invited us to guess
which of four holes it was, in a jug with four
handles to it, that the water poured from.
'Don't choose wrong,' she laughed, 'in case
you get a jet of water in your face.'
Only as we were parting from her was it
she showed us the right one, thanking us for our visit.
I gave a last look at the great
genius as he passed from sight,
telling myself: 'He manages here all right.'

[1947]   *(Donald Davie)*

How Soon...

How soon you take quite naturally
the leaves on all
the trees: how soon you take it naturally
that leaves fall;
how easily you take summer
and winter to be final;
how easily you would take
life to be eternal.

[1923–37, published 1949]
(William Jay Smith)

Complaint on Solipsism

Between myself and the apple tree
there stood my desire.
It was not the apple tree I saw –
But only my desire.
It was not the apple that I ate;
What I wished with all my soul –
An sich – has never been mine.

It is myself that I get back
from being's slot machine.
Wherever it is that my steps lead –
bits of my past come in the way
and not my future: That's why I'm poor
in an ever-rich today.

If only I had, in place of my head,
my liver instead –

[1938–39, published 1949]
(William Jay Smith)

It Is Five Years Now

It is five years now that you've been dead,
but from the grave you find your way –
nothing has changed – to the old café
where I waited for you, where last you waited
in the smoke-thatched gloom, in a corner where
you shivered as in some field lean-to;
the rain came down: we fought, we two;
and you were mad, but I didn't know then.

You're less than mad now; nothing has remained:
on the floor where time that danced so bright
has flown away, I sit mute, alone.
Absurd it is since you have gone:
the whole world seems to have gone mad –
and you, being mad, have won the fight.

[1942, published 1949]   *(William Jay Smith)*

Do You Remember?

Do you remember – when you were skating –
the long grass on the shallow
bottom, under a thin membrane
of ice; and the fish darting up below?

The green ice cracked: you raced ahead.
Around your foot there burst a star.
You raced ahead; with sparkling thunder,
racing with you, went the star.

You raced against danger: for as long
as you glided on ice you would not sink.
The braver you were, the safer by far:
safer always the greater the risk.

[1949]   (William Jay Smith)

In the Yellow House

I watched Napoleon lament,
the living Buddha vent his scorn
on Jesus, who, with sackcloth torn,
dug down into his excrement.

I saw a white straitjacket snarl,
its twisted face a riding crop
that beat its viewer to the pulp
it couldn't manage in a brawl.

Along those four forbidding halls,
what fallen creatures I could see
who'd shuffled off their sanity
and left it far outside those walls.

How well I understood all those
pains of Christ and Bonaparte
that felled my brothers at the start
and from which finally they rose.

But envy overcame me then
for somehow, casting off its weight,
the soul, rejecting its low state,
had made of them at last free men.

But I, compelled to carry on
the burden of my sanity –
who knows with what great agony
each human contact weighs me down.

My organs now have all declined
except for one that's firm: my brain;
no yellow house bears a deeper stain
than the one in which I am confined.

[1956]   *(William Jay Smith)*

Doleo Ergo Sum

My whole body aches. I feel it all; I ache, therefore,
I am. I laugh at this painful state that I detest.

I laugh to see that pain like a thoughtful host
Introduces my organs to me as my guests.

Lightning flashes along my bones and along my
    nerves:
With closed eyes, I come to know the places where it
    burns.

Each outcry, a handshake. I cry out, grimace –
And then shake hands with myself.

I didn't used to know where my larynx was nor the
    upper part of my lungs and liver
Nor this bulb that bangs so heavily in the back of my
    head.

Now I know everything that knocks, pinches, and
    bites –
The pains that light up in me like a row of lamplights.

Who knows only joy lives in a dream world; I feel
Ill but at least I am indeed the one who knows he is ill.

This is a great lesson I have learned. Who knows
What the world and life are like? Only those who have
    been made sick by them.

Who has known reality on this earth and the promise
    of truth beyond?
Only the poor and the suffering.

Who knows what the future will bring? Those acutely
    sensitive;
That is why even the healers come from those who
    are ill.

A sound bit of advice which forever in this world
    serves:
Leaders of nations, be the ganglions of burning
    nerves.

[1952]   *(William Jay Smith)*

Wild Geese

The wild geese, starting off on geometry
    over again,
acutely angle their initial faint
    wavering line.

Even today that simple diagram –
    and autumn – still
have strength to startle me as though I were
    a boy in school.

The floating diagrams are drawn again
    and rubbed off by
a secret and self-pleasing hand upon
    the blackboard-sky.

Watching this cryptic formula take shape
    the thousandth time,
I ask 'Why go?' and know no better now
    than on our farm.

Autumn meant leaving, for a different world,
    mother and home.
'You'll grow away from us.' From everything
    loved and well-known.

I took the message, went, and I am now
    as I turned out,
troubled by what I'll never understand –
    what I am not.

The wild geese, working rapidly, evolve
    their old designs,
and honk by, as they did when I was young,
    in drifting lines.

[1956]   (J. G. Nichols)

On Seeing the Reformation Monument, Geneva

I paced the length of it – one hundred and forty-three
paces from end to end. As a messenger
bearing the last salute of murdered millions
I passed along the line of stony faces;
Calvin, Knox, Farel, Beza! and those great bull-heads,
grim captains of embattled faith,
all those Williams, Colignys and Cromwells,
Bocskay with his battleaxe – how they looked at me!
It was all too much; I couldn't take them in!
I had to step back toward the garden, back
among the trees, back into the soul,
into that coolness where alone it is possible
to see a thing objectively and entirely.

And now, standing before me, at attention,
like so many soldiers on parade,
        they seemed almost
on the point of stepping forward
        out of the rock face
in which they stood,
out of Time, which had set
solidly at their backs.

Once they could move. Then they stiffened and
        became
stones in the sunlight. Their voices died away,
their words remain only in the form of deeds,
to provide a kind of explanation
somewhere in time... You who are dead,
you who stand at attention; speak!

        Or am *I* to speak first?

Must it always be with you as it always was –
'Here I stand; I can do no other.'
No compromise, whatever cause you serve,
for the lukewarm are spewed out of God's mouth,
while the right intention shall survive
like an object? How much truth is left
in those great fists which once, four centuries ago,
grasped a mighty oath and never once
released their grip, but stiffened into stone,
into eternity, their fingers still
grasping the Bible and the sword?
What did you think you saw
in the goal towards which you hastened,
pushing on with the rage of a lover
                as you drew near?
                    Do you sometimes wonder?
But suppose the answer should not be to your liking?
Well, I shall give it anyway.
It's just as bitter for me as it is for you.

You stood there, burning with the truth of God,
while the opposing camp burned with the same fire;
then, for the thousand-and-first time,
        instead of reason,
weapons and a flame resolved
how the soul may reach eternal bliss
Bodies writhed by the million
on battlefield and scaffold,
the wheel, the stake and all the new
master devices for inflicting pain;
and opposing forests,
forests of the cross of Jesus,
sprang up all over Europe. People burned,
in order that paintings, 'idols', should be burnt,
and the 'false Book' of the opposing party.
Cities and villages burned!
Half-savage mercenaries
devoured the flesh of men, fire met with fire,
crime with crime, until the final – Victory? –

Time, which awaited you, sagely, patiently,
with a touch of humour.
                    Now, today, in my country, as in yours,
the same two camps face each other still,
opposing fortresses gaze on opposing fortresses.
From ancient towers, austerely white or gold –
ornamented, opposing bells, like cannon,
peal out defiance to opposing bells,
every Sunday. And, inside, the priests
still thunder as they used to; but, after service
they wave across the street, signalling
at what time and at whose house this evening
they'll meet for a game of cards or a nice fish supper
with a few drinks.
                    Fair enough! I approve!
If I were a clergyman, I'd do the same!
'Live and let live' by all means.
                            And yet, you know –
those Thirty Years of Killing... wasn't it just
perhaps a little too high a price to pay?
D'Aubigné's fury, Coligny's death, the Night
of Saint Bartholomew still unavenged,
Germany, all Europe, torn apart,
and the Turk in our country
a hundred and fifty years...
So this was your 'victory'? God's way
of 'proving, like the sun', that the fight was not
for Him, but *because* of Him?
Was this the prize decreed to you by the future,
 – since there could have been no victor whom He
had not *predestined* to his triumph?
                            You won
The Devil won with you!
You were mugs, the lot of you! About turn!
You have no right to take even one step forward.
Crumble with your stone and with your Time –
Crumble! For the fight was lost before it had begun.
Or perhaps I spoke harshly, like one who first
castigates himself with his own truth.

So you failed.
The net result, written upon the blackboard –
– the continent you wiped clean with your armies –
was the mere answer to a foolish riddle,
and that only possible in Hungarian,
where Protestants call themselves 'keresztyén'
and Catholics call themselves 'keresztény'
both meaning 'Christian'. And so the riddle runs:
'Why is a keresztyén more than a keresztény?'
Did you really require the blood
of so many millions dead, before
you could distill this particle of sense,
this little 'y', and when, forgetful of
your duty, you took up the sword and hacked
the Gordian knot of Christian brotherhood,
(keresztyén hacking keresztény),
and when you had cut so valiantly,
through the tangle of your own perplexity,
did you find it there, that little 'y'?
And were you satisfied with your 'result'?

                          But suppose none of this
had ever been? Then only inside myself
the two opposing bells would toll,
calling up for the thousandth time
the old bitter conflict, hardly less bitter
for finding expression only in the old
vile opposition of two words; 'word-wrestling':
then the shepherd of Tolna
would have kept the faith of his old Lord;
then the preacher of Sárrét
Must have endured the battle – in his own breast.

What made you take up arms?
Does not a virtuous man in his own right
furnish a proper answer to the wicked?
And if the battle had not been fought? If, wordless,
the Faith had perished in 'the Roman Filth'?
If the world and the ideal together,

led by the 'Church vendor with the tiara',
had gone where it was no longer possible
to speak against unrighteousness? Well, of course,
it would have been indeed heroic to say:
'Here I stand; I can do no other!' Of course
virtue would have made its sacrifice!
but hopelessly! And what would then have happened
to us? Would we have been spared the conflict,
the bloody sacrifice, the Inquisition?
                              If – albeit 'in vain' –
Gustavus Adolphus had not ridden,
if the Puritans of Toulouse had chosen
to submit rather than take up arms,
if the Vaudois, the Hussites and the free men
of Bocskay, who knew no word of Scripture
nor yet of prayer, had said; 'We will not fight' –
do you suppose we should then have had peace?
I almost see a patronising smile
crossing your stony faces at the thought of it!
And would we Magyars have been quite the same
if there had been no Calvin?
                              I don't think so.

Or put it another way: would you have had
electric light, had not Giordano Bruno
gone to the stake? Here was the beginning
of nuclear power – and when, some time tomorrow,
you take a rocket and fly out into space,
you will have these to thank for it, men
who were not daunted by the stake or the galleys
        or the certain prospect of defeat,
the 'in vain' that waits on every step.
They saw: they saw it well,
that there is no road leading to the past;
the past collapsed in smoke, hurling them forward
as the powder hurls the cannon ball,
they undertook the burden of their Fate;
then say with me: Glory be to them!

I stood before them, a speechless messenger,
hardly caring now what explanation
their deeds might have to offer, deeds, which, like
a child, can be reasonable for themselves
only when they're grown up.
Finally, as a self-consolation, I said:
    Whoever was responsible for the intention,
not even God could have made it otherwise.

[1946–47, published 1956]   *(John W. Wilkinson)*

A Sentence for Tyranny

Where seek out tyranny?
There seek out tyranny,
Not just in barrels of guns,
Not just in prisons,

Not in the cell alone
Where third degree goes on,
Not in the night without
Challenged by sentry-shout,

Not where in deathbright smoke
Prosecutors' words provoke,
Not just in the emphasis
Of wall-tapped morse messages,

Not in confession told,
Not in the judge's cold
Death-sentence: 'Guilty!'
Not in the military

'Halt!' and the snapped-out 'Aim!'
'Fire!' and the drums of shame
Scattering the squad as it
Drags the corpse to the pit,

Not in the furtively
Guarded, and fearfully
Breathed words the message bore
Passed through half-open door,

Not in the 'Hush!' revealed
On mouth by finger sealed,
Nor confine tyranny yet
To rigid features set,

70

Peering through bars that still
Show, through that iron grille,
Cries that dumb throats retract,
Stopped in the cataract

Of inarticulate tears
Deepening the silent fears
in pupils griefs dilate
Darkened by looming fate,

Not only in 'Viva!' cries
Track down all tyrannies,
Surging on tiptoe, strong,
In the acclaiming song.

Where seek out tyranny?
There seek out tyranny,
Not just in mustered bands,
Tirelessly clapping hands,

Fanfares, and opera stalls;
Just as crude, just as false,
Monuments, art galleries,
Though cast in stone, speak lies:

Yes, each framed lie can crush.
Even in the painter's brush,
Or in the car with slight
Noise gliding through the night,

Where it draws up and waits
Throbbing in front of gates,
There, omnipresent, not
Less than your ancient God,

There seek out tyranny,
In school, in nursery,
In father's guiding rule
And in the mother's smile,

In, where a stranger puts
Questions that touch the roots,
Answering the stranger's gaze,
What the child always says;

Not just where barbed wire twines,
Not just between book-lines,
More than in barbed wire, in
Slogans that prick your skin:

There, more discreet, it is
In a wife's parting kiss,
Near you and at your back:
'When, dear, will you be back?'

In words that folk repeat,
'How d'you do's in the street,
Sudden, then, in the softer
Handshake a moment after

Making your lover's face
Found in the meeting-place
Freeze on the instant
Because it is present,

Not in the interrogation
Only, but love's confession,
In the words' honeyed wine
Like a fly in the wine,

For even in your dreams
You are preceded:
It had entered the bridal bed
And the desire it bred;

There's nothing you think fair
It has not already claimed;
Your bed it stole to share
Even when love was named:

It is in the plate, the glass,
In the nose and the mouth,
It is in the cold and the dark,
In the outer air and in your house;

As if through an open window
Came the reek of carrion
Or as if in the house there was
Somewhere a leak of gas.

Talk to yourself and hear
Tyranny your inquisitor;
You have no isolation,
Not even in imagination.

Through it the Milky Way becomes
A frontier terrain, scoured by beams,
A minefield, and the star
A spy-hole in a war.

The swarming canopy of the sky
Is a monstrous labour camp:
The Orator Tyranny
Speaks from bells on the ramp;

From the priest, to whom you confess,
From his sermon no less;
Church, Parliament, these
And the rack, are but stage properties:

Open and close your eyes;
Still its scrutiny lies
Upon you like a sickness,
Following you with memory's quickness.

Hark at the wheels of the train;
This is their refrain:
'You're a prisoner, prisoner, cast into jail
        by the binder.'
on the hill, by the sea, you inhale the same
        reminder.

In the lightning flash it is seen,
In every unforeseen
Little noise; its dart
Lights up your astonished heart.

Where you rest, there it is
In boredom's manacles,
In showers that forge nearby
Bars that reach up the sky,

In the snow, whose fall
Sheer as a cell wall
Hides you while tyranny looks
Through the eyes of your dog,

For it is in all you intend,
In your to-morrow it is at hand,
Before your thoughts it is aware,
In your every movement it is there;

As water cleaves the river-bed
You follow and form it: but instead
Of peering from that circle anew,
Out of the glass it looks at you.

In vain you try to escape its wrath:
Prisoner and jailer, you are both;
It works its own corrosive way
Into the taste of your tobacco,

Into the very clothes you wear –
It penetrates you to the marrow;
Detach your sense from it, you find
No other thought will come to your mind.

You look about, but what prompts your
    gazing?
You use your eyes, but what do they catch?
Already a forest fire is blazing
Fanned into flame by the stick of a match

Where carelessly you threw it down
As you walked, and forgot to tread it in,
And now it guards you in the town,
In field and home and the factories' din;

No longer you feel what it is to live;
Bread and meat, you do not know them;
You cannot have desire, nor love;
To stretch out your arms is now denied you.

Thus the slave forges with care
The fetters he himself must wear;
You nourish tyranny when you eat;
You beget your child for it.

Where seek tyranny? Think again:
Everyone is a link in the chain;
Of tyranny's stench you are not free:
You yourself are tyranny.

Like a mole on a sunny day
Walking in his blind, dark way,
We walk and fidget in our rooms,
Making a Sahara of our homes;

All this because, where tyranny is,
Everything is in vain,
Every creation, even this
Poem I sing turns vain:

Vain, because it is standing
From the very first at your grave,
Your own biography branding,
And even your ashes are its slave.

[1951, published 1956]
(Vernon Watkins)

Bartók

'Harsh discord?' – Yes! They think it thus
which brings us solace!
Yes! Let the violin strings,
let singing throats
learn curse-clatter of splintering glass
crashing to the ground
the screen of rasp
wedged in the teeth
of buzzing saw; – let there be no peace, no gaiety
in gilded, lofty far
and delicate, closed-off concert halls,
until in woe-darkened hearts!

'Harsh discord!' Yes! They think it thus
which brings us solace!
that the people live
and have still a soul,
their voice is heard! Variations on the curse
of steel grating crashing against stone
Though on the tuned and taut
piano and vocal cords
to stark existence their bleak truth,
for this same 'harsh discord',
this woeful battle-cry disturbing hell's infernal din
cries out
Harmony!
For this very anguish cries out
– through how many falsely sweet songs – and
shouts
to fate: Let there be Harmony,
order, true order, or the world is lost,
the world is lost, if the people
speak not again – in majesty!

O stoic, stern musician, true Magyar
(like many of your peers – 'notorious')
was it ordained by law, that from the depth
of the people's soul, whither you descended
through the trumpet, the as yet mine-shaft throat
of this pit, you should send up the cry
into this frigid-rigid giant hall
whose soft-lights myriad candles are?

Frivolous, soothing melodies played in my ear
insult my grief:
let no light-tuned Zerkovicz sing the dirge at this,
our mother's funeral;
homelands are lost – who dares to mourn them
with grind-organ arpeggios?
Is there hope yet in our human race?
If this be our care and the reeling brain battles
benumbed, speak, you
fierce, wild, severe, aggressive great musician,
that – for all that! – we still have cause
to hope, to live,

And that we have the right
– for we are mortals and life-givers –
to look all that in the eye
which we may not avoid.
For troubles grow when they are covered.
It was possible, but no more,
to hide our eyes, to cover our ears
while storms wreak their havoc,
and later revile: you did not help!

You do us honour by revealing what
is revealed to you,
the good, the bad, virtue and sin –
you raise our stature by
speaking to us as equals.
This – this consoles!
What different words are these!
Human, not sham.
It gives us the right; and so the strength to face
the harshest despair.

Our thanks for it,
for the strength to take victory
even over hell.

Behold the end that carries us on.
Behold the guidon: by speaking out
the horror is dissolved.
Behold the answer to life's riddle
by a great mind, an artist's spirit: it was worth suffering
through hell.

Because we have suffered such things that still
there are no verbs for them,
Picasso's two-nosed women,
six-legged stallions
alone could have keened abroad
galloping, neighed out
what we have borne, we men,
what no one who has not lived it can grasp,
for which there are no words now, nor can be perhaps,
only music, music, music, like your music
twin lodestars in our sky of sound,
music alone, music alone, music,
hot with ancient breath of mine-depths,
dreaming 'the people's future song',
nursing them to triumph,
setting them free so that the very walls
of prisons are razed,

for bliss promised, here on earth
praying with blasphemy,
sacrificing with sacrilege,
wounding to cure,
music now lifting
worthy listeners to a better world –

work, a good healer, who lulls not to sleep;
who, probing our soul
with your chord-fingers, touches
where trouble lies,
and how strange, how wholesome is the salve you give:
the plaintive call,
the lament which would spring from us,
but cannot spring,
for we are born to dumb stillness of heart:
your nerve strings sing for us.

[1956]   *(Claire Lashley)*

Grass Snake and Fish

Among pebbles, at the pond's edge,
    in limpid shallows whose water
flows as transparent as the atmosphere,
    suddenly visible

in that world made for other lungs,
    living purity, where
the stone wavers in the drift
    of the reflection, a branch in air;

into that shut Eden, slides the snake,
    guided by the oldest law:
a fish palpitates hanging from its fangs
    howling what no one can translate.

[1956]   *(Charles Tomlinson)*

Consolation

Your sorrow overflowed you; I let the stream
running across the pebbles
bathe my hands; and that
was how I heard you.

Clear, the water glided
between my fingers, time
without color fled
almost alive, between my fingers.

I listened to time
caressing my palms and
murmuring out its flight:
it was your flowing sorrow I handled.

I was sad... and yet
already beneath the bruising
of spent time, my hands
foretold appeasement.

[1961]   *(Charles Tomlinson)*

Charon's Boat

Our trip in Charon's boat does not begin that day
When eyes are closed in everlasting sleep:
Aware and open-eyed, we transients sail away
Across the fateful deep.

Long years before our envious fate embarked upon
The journey ultimate – of no return –
The ship, responding to our every whim, sailed on,
Wonder at every turn.

Past beautiful canals, mysterious lagoons, –
Familiar route, as if we had rehearsed;
The sky, the gentle landscape, fit for honeymoons –
All scenes are in reverse!

And all is fresh and lovely; more intriguing
The pictures, as before our eyes they spin;
Just as a tune is sweeter upon leaving
The singing violin.

We sit among the trees, with friends we gaily laugh –
When suddenly the boat begins to rock;
The time has come for us – an end to talk and chaff –
We recognize the knock.

He is a sage, who on this trip accepts his fate;
Who smiles, or weeps with tears of gratitude,
For all the treasures he has shared of late,
During his Interlude.

[1956, published 1961]   (Marie B. Jaffe)

A Sad Guest

An old beggar in the wintertime
staggering in the doorway of a hut,
standing there speechless, happy
    happy he's not left out,
happy he's in at last, inside!
God came to me like this at times.

A sad guest, always tearful, shivering.
Faith? That's what he begged for.
We shared it. Then, as the sky grew milder,
    he offered his hand,
  and accepted what I gave.
Waiting outside were madmen, murderers, and priests.

[1961]   *(John Batki)*

For Calmness

Rain at the end of spring and black cloud,
and a fire in the stove still needed
in a house pushed by the mountain wind
where I survived to the winter's end,
where the stove is cold; my overcoat
is hardly keeping the weather out.
Bones and coat against the window-sill,
I suffer the edge to penetrate
as if to distract my sickened heart
which questions why I should live at all.

The fierce rumblings of Lake Balaton
shake the dusk; its fanged rush leaps along
to burn mad-houses, to raze the sties,
force pent-up screaming and the harsh cries
of a goaded monkey-pack. At times
words I can understand in the din:
a human voice but filling the sky
shouts, 'Hurry!' then choking, 'After him!'
then, 'Look out!' then louder still, 'Why try!'
then laughing, 'You helped it to happen!'

The storm's tumbling cacophonies cross
the sequences I seek, the statements
I listen for: these thrown voices are
mirrors flashing, mirrors that I hear,
reflecting with sudden prophecy.
What do they show us? What kind of face
wavering from the despondency
and numbing cold of the soul's blind base?

Inside and outside aching alike
over the ruins, Carthage, a life
breaking beyond my reparation;
and rattling round its celebration
my poem, tensed, a frenzied shaman
but praying for calmness to come down.

[1965]   *(Alan Dixon)*

Mother Sun

After the artificial warmth of wood
and coal, a stepmother's measured
warmth which, like our daily bread,
we have to earn sweating, how good

this udder-warmth is, this milk-warmth
that the central heating of the sun,
burning again, causes to run
into bent vessels of blood and lymph.

All my pores drink it greedily.
This is what is really free,
pouring into us, thick and fast as ever!

It permeates me so, so much grace
makes me believe we must, in some place,
have an eternal mother.

[1965]   *(Anthony Edkins)*

A World in Crystal

Each leaf on the tree becomes
        a transparency of crystal,
brown and purple porcelain,
        ivory in places.
The trees hold forth their
        tiny Japanese cups;
they do not move for fear
        a single one might fall.

The orchard's filled with light;
        everything there trembles:
it's a shop that offers lamps
        and crystal ornaments.
"Take care," my heart tells me
        in secret, "not to break
some sparkling object there
        with your clumsy gesture."

And yet what perfect pleasure,
        what pure childish joy
it was to shake the trees
        and to remain beneath
that shower of gold; and then
        how wonderful to drown,
to die within that light
        and colour pouring down.

Now furtively I stroll
        among the cherry trees
with their Japanese red tea
        service of porcelain.
All detachable beauty
        causes me pain. I live

in fear for all the fragile
     values of this earth.

A transparency of crystal
     exists not just in trees,
transparency is all:
     faces, hearts of air –
all transparency –
     tell me, will you, how
well in autumn wind
     will fragile being fare?

The wind has not yet risen;
     creation and the garden
stand clearly in the light.
     All the more painful now
to watch, as here and there,
     from high in a still tree
– and in what deathly silence –
     a crystal leaf drifts down.

[1959, published 1961]
     (William Jay Smith)

Aboard the Santa Maria

A dirty fog is swirling in the wake
Of a lonely house perched out above the lake.

The trunk of a tall fir tree stands, a mast,
but even its very tip in the fog is lost.

Buttressed forth, a hanging garden there,
the terrace like a ship divides the air.

A table of stone, a rickety chicken coop
emerge through holes within the shifting fog;

and farther on, a friend withdrawing from the road,
a *ritirato* made of pre-Columbian wood.

And now when the pounding waves reach up to me,
I feel I am centuries ago at sea.

On some Santa Maria I sail off through the air,
but I, its master, am wondering to where.

Lurching up and down the deck I go,
drugged by medicine, not alcohol.

We speed ahead: tatters of fog flutter and play
in the trees, signals that time is speeding away.

And now and then a gull sweeps through the fog –
but black it is; and crows a pitiful caw.

[1965]   (William Jay Smith)

Logbook of a Lost Caravan

Only the compass, keeping hope alive,
    stuttered on, uttering its paralyzed
directions; with something somewhere beyond
    to which to respond.

    And for another long day
we struggled ahead through desert sand.

Then to the edge of stone cliffs
    covered with hieroglyphs.

Line after line, incoherent, they read –
    wrinkles on some mad forehead.

    An ancient age
struggled there in desperate tones –

With nothing more to say –

    And only the wind moans.

Sand in our eyes. Between sweating fingers, and
    ground between teeth, sand.

We slaughtered the camel who knew the way...
    had our final meal today.

[1965]   *(William Jay Smith)*

Tilting Sail

The tilting sail careens;
    scything the foam,
the tall mast creaks and leans –
    the boat plows on.

Look – when do mast and sail
    fly forward most
triumphantly? When tilted
    lowest.

[1965]   *(William Jay Smith)*

A Record

It was easy then to catch
the flow of a stream: it murmured
at once through the pulsing
rhythms of my poems –
the mountain, the meadow – whatever
our words touched took human form.

But then came the bleak
country; the Alps of slag,
the barren soul of mining
towns, lunar gray.
The waste from tanneries,
hell-born, black as the Styx.
Red-brick barracks
through which again and again –
like the striking of obstinate, mad
clocks – crackled firing squads.

And then this:
purple smoke and ash
floating in place of sky
over a land of chimneys
thicker than vineyard poles.

And we recorded this:
for here our forces passed,
children and dogs at our heels,
bent more and more by the weight
of our useless belongings.

[1965]   (William Jay Smith)

93

Ruler

I wanted without delay to give order to the world, so I first put my boxes in order, then my votive pictures, then my stamps. The latter I considered most effective in carrying my will even to the most insignificant islands in the farthest parts of the world. What purpose, what peace of mind, what plans – at the end of each day! What good will!

Nor was ruthlessness alien to me. Whose eyes blink less at the sight of death and torture than a tyrant's? A child's.

And what pleasure in granting pardon!

At Simontornya, on the far bank of the Sió, in the Dzindzsa quarter, before the open oven door in a peasant kitchen, with an album of my own making opened in my lap, when spring had already released its clouds on a still cold sky. On the side of Mózsé Hill – the name of everything there was unique – yes, then it was...

Today, exiled – dethroned, and even ushered out of my own mausoleum – I weep for the magic of lost power.

[1965]   *(William Jay Smith)*

Brazilian Rain Forest

In Old Buda, a street almost as wide as a square coming down from Újlaki Church. The one-storey houses here are even lower than usual. The pavement once swelled to the level of the windows, and remained there as in some frozen flood. From such a house, a tavern still privately owned, a tall slender young woman who is well-dressed comes out into the Friday twilight. Her eyes are glazed; she is dead drunk. She sways gracefully. The basalt cobble-stones of the broad street mock her by pretending to be the stepping stones across a mountain stream, and that's why she may only step on every second one. Since the stones are wet, the scene is made all the more probable. It is raining, fully and evenly, as in the tropics, although it is November. The pouring rain is broken into threads by the light of the street lamps. The woman's dishevelled hair drips also into so many threads. She is soaked to the skin.

She is soaked to the skin, but does not feel a thing.

Otherwise she would not push away the threads of rain as if she were parting the reeds of a marsh or thrusting aside the bead curtain of some southern barber shop. But after this bead curtain comes another and then another, ten, twenty, a hundred, thousand upon wondrous thousand.

All this, of course, is illusion. The situation and reality: the woman walks amid the lianas, the hanging tendrils of a Brazilian rain forest, and above her are trees teeming with bright-colored parakeets, snarling monkeys, serpents, and other creatures that do not even exist in South America, but have come here only for this occasion. At such a time who would not think of coming to her aid? As Chateaubriand says, this is how the most exciting adventures with native women really begin. Yes, but there is something rarely taken into account – the distances in a rain forest! Between the two of us, my sailor's eye tells me, a thousand miles at least.

[1962–1965]   *(William Jay Smith)*

Deliverance

I remember how one winter morning, as clear as water, in order to see us all the better that great blue eye opened above us in the mountain cabin. I went out on the balcony. The air – oh, purifying presence! – was frozen, and the sharp blades of its rays shone. The delicate ice crystals were volcanos of light along the grass, the branches, on the slopes of the valley and on the confiding hills which, wishing to bring themselves from the past into the future, had begun to move towards us. Everything around us extended its promise. You love me. On a sky wide enough to make one lose one's memory floated a single bird, and it was naturally black. This was the last sin, the last moment when one could feel guilty. It is not without reason that the words "breath" and "soul" in Hungarian have the same root. A breath can sometimes change the soul. I have flown off and I am back, as happy as a sick man who has been operated on and cured.

[1962–1965]   *(William Jay Smith)*

The Approaching Silence

Lightly clad, on tiptoe, the little rain has just run into the garden through the gate. Is the sunlight here? The rain stops, listens, gazing at itself in the glass balls, shifts its weight; draws away. But it is still here; now and then its drops continue to fall.

Whom is it looking for? The plants have now all resumed their allegiance to the sun; the wettest enjoy the light with all the more brilliance. Yet there is one fewer bird, one fewer, now singing. That one has got wind of things; he is sharp. Or can it be mere politeness?

I am old, and feel even older, sensing how light is the passing of the rain. Another bird stops. I sense even this slight encore of silence. A silence that feels close even though already part of all that is boundless. But it creates a stage for what light graces around one who darkens and grows heavy.

[1965]   (William Jay Smith)

Early Darkness

Before autumn's swift clouds the moon bounds to and
fro, wishing to see itself reflected in the cool well water
before departing – torn away. It holds out like an obsti-
nate woman, but not for long. The corn shucks rattle.
After the mad chase, the last hare sits on its haunches,
pricks up its ears, and gradually stiffens into sculpture as
catastrophe approaches.

[1965]   (William Jay Smith)

Putting Things in Order

The thin blade of the sword on which I absently fell –
taking pains that its point touch my heart – that gentle
blade has pierced me through and through. And then?
Everything fell obediently into place. The landscape
turned cold. Leaves contracted like the hands of misers
and, emptied, fell. A careful wind came, even returning
for bits it had left behind. Towards evening a ship
passed but by that time the entire area had long been
barren stone. And the last natives, what purpose do
they serve? The same as the bedouins one sees with
their camels in those pictures of the Egyptian pyramids:
to give a sense of proportion to the lingering and now
cosmic sadness.

[1965]   *(William Jay Smith)*

Work

They stuck pigs in the throat. Might I not have done it myself? They tossed chickens with their heads cut off out into the courtyard. With a child's thirst for knowledge, I watched their final spasms with a heart hardly touched. My first really shattering experience came when I watched the hooping of a cartwheel.

From the huge coal fire, with pincers at least a yard long, the apprentices grabbed the iron hoop, which by then was red hot up and down. They ran with it to the fresh-smelling oak wheel that had been fixed in place in the front of the blacksmith's shop. The flesh-colored wooden wheel was my grandfather's work; the iron hoop, which gave off a shower of sparks in its fiery agony, was my father's. One of the apprentices held the sledge hammer, the other the buckets. Places, everyone. As on shipboard. As at an execution. The hoop, which in its white-hot state had just expanded to the size of the wheel, was quickly placed on it; and they began to pry it out with their tongs. My father swung the hammer with lightning speed, giving orders all the while. The wood caught fire; they poured a bucket of water on it. The wheel sent up steam and smoke so thick you couldn't see it. But still the hammer pounded on, and still came the 'Press hard'! uttered breathlessly from the corner of the mouth. The fire blazed up again.

Water flung again as on a tortured man who has sunk into a coma. Then the last flourishing bush of steam evaporated while the apprentices poured a thin trickle from a can on the cooling iron which, in congealing, gripped lovingly its life-long companion to be. The men wiped the sweat from their brows, spat, shook their heads, satisfied. Nothing – not the slightest flicker of a movement – could have been executed differently.

[1965]   (William Jay Smith)

While the Record Plays

They heated hatchet blades over gas fires in roadside
   workshops and hammered them into cleavers.

They brought wooden blocks on trucks and carried
   them across these new provinces grimly, quickly,
   and steadily: almost according to ritual.

Because at any time – at noon or midnight – they would
   arrive at one of these impure settlements,

where women did not cook nor make beds as theirs
   did, where men did not greet one another as they
   did, where children and the whole damned com-
   pany did not pronounce words as they did, and
   where the girls kept apart from them.

They would select from these insolent and intolerable
   people twelve men, preferably young ones, to take
   to the marketplace,

and there – because of *blah-blah-blah* and moreover
   quack-quack-quack and likewise *quack-blah-quack*
   – would beat and behead them,

of historical necessity – because of *twaddle-twiddle* and
   twiddle-diddle, and expertly, for their occupations
   would be different one from the other,

agronomist and butcher, bookbinder and engineer,
   waiter and doctor, several seminarists, cadets from
   military academies, a considerable number of stu-
   dents,

those familiar with Carnot, Beethoven and even
   Einstein, displaying their finest talents,

because, after all, nevertheless, *blah-blah-blah* and
   twiddle-dee-dee,

while through loudspeakers records played – music and
   an occasional gruff order, and they, the zealous
   ones, wiped their foreheads and turned aside
   every now and then to urinate since excitement
   affects the kidneys;

then having washed the blocks and hauled down the
   large tricolor which on such occasions always
   waved above their heads,

they too would march on into the broad future,

past the heads, carefully placed in a circle,

then out of the settlement where now also

and forever and ever,

reason, comfort, and hope would be no –

wrr-wrr-wrr – that is to say – *we-ep, wa-rp,* the sound (by
   now the only one without music or words) that the
   needle makes as the record grinds on.

[1965]   *(William Jay Smith)*

Ode to a Lawgiver

A Jubilee greeting to Tersánszky

The law could be right and valid for everyone,
If we human beings could be cast
Like adobes by the billion
From the same mould, the first one like the last.

But what must be must be;
Every heart has its separate way,

And for some time now,
We have been more than clay and clay.

I will be plain, as only a writer can,
In whom the scholar and the judge are one,

And sing of something new.

Let there be law, a living law
In which all men cohere and none conflict,

Whose total force may draw
The partial truth of one, yet not restrict
The movement of the one within the whole
– As an adobe in a mould – but let
Each, like an atom, freely circulate,
In its own sphere within the general soul.

Existence should create order, not sorrow!

All power, then, to the shade, whose form
May hold the blueprint of tomorrow,
To the exception
From which tomorrow's rule may follow
And to the poet, the man most fit
To experiment; let him be free for this,
Does it require less talent than to seek out
A cure for cancer? Less
Creative zeal
Than to harness the atom's power to a driving wheel
Or cross the brink of outer space,
To discern, ripening in the mind,

The form of future days,

To lay bare, as with ultra-violet rays
Tomorrow's rule for all mankind
Outlined in embryo?
What the nerves apprehend but cannot know?

This from the distance of a milliard years!

All power to the surgeon's knife
Which turns back the false surface and lays bare the
life,
Separating each minute the bare tissue
From the live,
Putting things right, alert for every issue,
Every latent force, whence may derive
This man's murder
That man's thievishness,
How beauty is deformed,
How the deformed grows beautiful,
Whether he who is termed
'Leader' is a hero or a clod –

Since there's no royal road
To acceptance in our time;
So many curious facts emerging –
Words from the dumb,
The hunter being pursued,
The lewd woman a virgin
And the virgin lewd.

Not all creative beings are like that,
But I believe that those who must proceed
And fight after this fashion, are the ones
Whose formations we most need
To watch for, the reconnaissance
In whom tomorrow's battle lines appear.
Before them, Anna Karenina, Bánk, Hamlet
Dance like flames in the upper air,
Fantastically clear.

The ancient world takes on a rare
Lustre from their tones.

All hail! then, to those who bear
Law and light within their bones,

Men who will face the stake, the mocker's sneer,
Even failure – and still press on,
Whether they quite know why or not.

Let us salute Jenő Tersánszky, then,
For the journey he made and the truth he brought.

Vivat!

Sing on, master of many voices! Build
Your collapsible dinghies, plan
Your ancient reed pipes, new brakes for bicycles, gild
Your divinely useless gadgets,
Your total man
In all his crazy details!

Never take your arms and mind and mouth from the
task.
Long may you work, be happy! But take care,
That – like this century – you never ask
Who you are!

[1965]   *(John W. Wilkinson)*

To the Trees

Now, at last, you must leave us, dear companions,
trees, the sharers of our summer joys,
the slender poplar and the portly walnut
who drank with us the gold of sunlit days,
hornbeams, beeches, nourished by the sky
from the same kitchen as ourselves, who were
our foster-brothers, not in milk but light,
brothers in heat and soil, cloud, matter, air,
loyal homeland trees, the alarms of parting
are at hand; showers of sharp steel
needles have come whirling down since morning,
flung out, from the snowstorm's giant wheel!
Snowstorm! Twenty degrees of frost! The meadow
heaves in chalkwhite waves, all creatures run
who can; the sudden flood drains from the landscape
as sudden-swiftly as it had begun:
men run as if they were drowning; the house is now
an island (a southern one if heated!) the dog
sits and howls on the snow-foamy threshold
and flocks of birds take refuge in the stack.
Only you, the trees, stand out unshaken
in the chalkwhite sea, this moonscape which
stabs us to the lungs, bites like a dagger
into our inmost flesh, but cannot reach
you, happy amphibians, who endure
this other element, able to breathe
what (like the atmosphere of outer space
or the pre-human earth) would mean our death.
You button up your cloaks of bark around you,
you send your tepid bloodstream spreading through
from the limbs, the crown and down the trunk
into the root, and what is it to you
how far this planet strays from the sun's circle
into what cold? you – who know what awaits

all life on this grim soil, ruled by necessity –
merely suspend existence when it hurts!
Heroic, primeval strikers! For where's the sense
in living otherwise than without pain?
Tenacious ones! You have always won through the
      frost,
to see the snow melt round your feet again.
...It is sad to leave you, full grown trees! bushes!
hedges! Though ice tinkles and hoar-frost glares from
your branches, I feel you growl defiance;
you live, like denizens of other stars!
wise brothers who turned to other paths, or, like
so many Abels, kept to the old roads,
 – true to the same old faith, 'one flock, one
      shepherd' –
whom Cain's accursed breed murders, denudes
and may exterminate at last, in order
day by day to place a log upon
the stolen fire of its own shivering race...
mutilated corpses every one!

[1965]   *(John W. Wilkinson)*

Old Men Pursued

Away Tolstoy began to run,
not from death.

Did he run down

from the summits,
the same direction as Móricz
whose old stick took a new lease
of life? He taught prevention of frost. He'd say
make your own bricks, show his peasants the way.

'If there is some small thing that I can save.'

Old men, like saints
touched by an angel on the shoulder,
sent on your way, but with what order?
How? Never against

your own wishes.
Who could compel you?
Whose message tell you
to forget yourselves?
No word from a god, or doctrine
of fear made you run
from your fellow-man
to know his house and bad fortune.

We are reminded of student days
and the smell of winter ending; youngsters,
moon-governed, our noses bled with regularity:
now we are drawn to the valleys, disturbed
by perching on the heights,
seeing the breathless way ascended.
The fields and houses below, where death is known
as an animal is known.

I will not hold my hat and stick
too easily when I must take
the down direction when a whistle blows;
led by my dogs, my oddities,
my happy pack
of barking fools!...

[1968]   (Alan Dixon)

The Maker

1

Like a voyeur
I watched their coming together
among the springs,
the watchmaker's gaze
of pointed steel, and
his tweezers –
the way they were testing one another!

It was all explained to me in advance,
anxiously I watched
as under the cover of a blue flame
in the test-tube, two thoughts
of the chemist were gladly becoming
better acquainted.

A stirring among the golden springs,
a tentative whirr of a new creature
trying its wings,
teetering on the twigs
of the nest's rim.

More ardent
than two lithe bodies dancing
together, embracing,
those two
thoughts so different from each other
frolicked and turned
struggling
for life, for death,

finding their fulfilment
in a third.

2

As a babe in the hands of a midwife
begins to live, a success,
tiny, naked,
powerful,
it kicked among the wheels and springs,
a deed that has been given
life and body almost
like our own.
It came with me,
came as my perpetual
dog, my master
on my leash,
myself on leash.

3

With eyes more screwed-up than an ant's,
on the nib of my pen
it turns, spying
on my work –
it lurks, waiting to find
a gap,
a split-second only, to rush
through space
exchanging its message
for another.

Glistening,
the file slid back and forth;
shrieking as though
by its own light,
the copper rod, thick
as a finger in the vise;
jammed,
jumped, it too
wanted to do something
by itself.

Then from that oily palm
like a tiny fish
rushing with purpose from the instant of its birth,
it wanted to leap
among companions,
into its element,

knowing its place from the start.

5

What a fate. We have no
director to guide us, no
thread to follow, only
this work in our hand,

this quivering little compass.

This is the oldest
god, a dog sniffing
the long trail to where we are

from the time when islands
floated and the mountains rose
ever so slowly,
as though to show there is direction:
an order needs something
more than itself,

needs companions.

6

What humiliation!
What a spur to pride,
that the premiere bit of good counsel
for our far-famed human
mind – to tell the truth its
most brilliant argument – was
the original gift of
the exchanges between
the two thumbs and the index
fingers...

7

Nothing's sweeter than the ecstasy
of such revenge!
No god, no leader
protects me,
only that ardor,
frailer than an inchworm
at my fingertip
– what does it accomplish? –
to set
something right.

This purpose
is no longer mine alone,
this challenge
risen from the dust, that says
go on, and

the stars will change places!

– By our will.

8

To grasp the first clue
of a puzzle, the neck of a net,
the purpose of my being alive here on earth,
of my servitude,
from what work whispers to me,
and then the network of the planets,

whatever is confused, obscure
even in the tissue of the light,
or in my mind,
– that is servitude; perdition;
dying.

To stand face to face, to grapple
head on like a pair of wrestlers
locked in the fight to the death, yes,
to fight it out with
death, with
fear,
although smeared with mud, to carry to safety
something pure.

The order, the order that suits me.

9

What poverty is this,
what wealth,
never to have known a handshake
more stirring to the heart,
more stimulating than the touch
of the gods
– it was no longer my hand guiding
hammer and wedge
but them mine.

10

Well, I create too.
I can make things.
Since then, the Rival hasn't shown
his spectral face.

Jealous, eh? Put to shame?
That time I had to spread the sheaf of reeds
between four stakes to make a roof,
the heavens began to fall,
tumbling, thundering, uncontrollable –

fell in hail on the first garden.

That now is lost.

But not the eternal craving for it,
nor the memory of it.

All the mines, blast furnaces, atomic piles
of Europe, America, all the continents
and planets yet to be reached
in the future
cannot squeeze
into one fist as much power, as much knowledge
as you,
the first

to swing an axe-handle,
sky-crushing.

How sad it is to be an orphan,
to have no step-father
but the one I raise.

It is pitiable to be alone,
the one whom nobody can love
but she whom I can teach
how to love.

Facing nothingness,
hell simmering with its secrets?
The labyrinth of our fears.
Taking in hand, at last, slowly,
assiduously, moving well,
our face, too,
the divine.
The one which faces itself.

In our children
reunited.

13

With these mortal eyes
to learn what I am here to do,
the job that waits for me to do it,
for which somewhere,
a peasant, hoeing, sends me this
glass of wine,
a worker touching down his soldering-iron
sent light
into my room,
to find with mortal eyes
the eternal task:
Make the future speak!
– already it is quarreling with death,

skillfully, intelligent,
bustling, with
authority.

To do the job
well, to our liking
– yes, like good
love-making.

Almost stroking its face
in gratitude.

To leave it there,
to look back a few times
on the one who lies there satisfied;
she keeps my riches,
conceiving my future,
the meaning, maybe forever, of all
I was here for,

mortal, imperishable.

[1968] *(Daniel Hoffman)*

Congress Flags

Menton, Before the Storm

Fiercely fluttering flags, many-tongued
flags of fifty countries, line the roofs!
Waving their different colours, Iceland,
Finland and Japan shout their truths!

Inside the hall, what delegates decide
carries the world's trademark of power.
Outside above the marble façade
there's equality, for each banner.

One fate for all. One wind the same
way giving orders – left turn! right turn! –
and Great Britain's covered now and again
by its Chilean neighbour.

Cloth writhing on poles that are the same
proclaims different lands have but one passion,
regardless which of them inflame
the most hearts – perhaps towards annihilation.

'Poles and cloth, poles and cloth' – but not
just poles, just cloth! – when wind starts blowing
Pentecostal flames of tongues flare up – what
Babel-babbling!

Yet even this Babel's maddened chatter
says something: a longing, longing, what longing
for this many-tongued world to utter
one message in common.

Along the rows the eye wanders – where
is the one which stirred our immature heart?
For many it's the same when it's there –
for none when it is not.

[1970]   (Kenneth McRobbie)

A Wreath

You can no longer
soar. And yet you blaze,
wind-slit Hungarian tongue, sending
your snakelike flames along the ground, hissing
at times with pain,
more often with the helpless rage of the humiliated,
your guardian angels forsaking you.

Again in grass,
in weeds, in slime.
As through all those centuries, among
the stooped peasants. Among
the tight-lipped old, keeping their counsel. Among
girls trembling under coned reeds as
the Tartar hordes swept past. Among
children lashed together
while mute lips shaped their words,
for the Turks, if they heard a sound,
would bring whips down in their faces.
Now you show forth
truly – and to me as well – your use,
your pedigree, your coat-of-arms, the stone-biting
strength in your veins.

Language of furtive smiles,
of bright tears shared in secret, language
of loyalty, lingo
of never-surrendered faith, password of hope, language
of freedom, briefly-snatched freedom, behind-the-
prison-guard's-back-freedom,
language of master-mocked schoolboy, sergeant-
abused rookie,
dressed-down plaintiff, of little old ladies boring clerks,

language of porters, odd-job hired men, being a
    language
of the no-good-for-the-factory, no-good-for-test-passing
    proletariat,
language of the veteran stammering before his
young boss; testimony –
rising from depths even greater
than Luther's – of the suspect
beaten up on arrival at the station;
language of the Kassa black marketeer, the Bucharest
    servant girl,
the Beirut whore, all calling
for mother, behold your son, spittle
on his rage-reddened face,
master of many tongues,
held worthy of attention by other nations
for what, as a loyal European,
he has to say:
he cannot mount any festive platform,
cannot accept any wreath,
however glorious, which he would not, stepping
    quickly down,
carry over to lay at your feet, and with his smile draw
    forth,
on your agonizing lips,
your smile, my beloved, ever-nurturing mother.

[1972]   *(William Jay Smith)*

Night Watch

A small but persistent pain
in the gums, in the windpipe,
in the brain.
In the thicket of the intestines.
A enemy scout scans to see
where the army can invade –
cancer, a stroke or the third heart attack.
The old people cock their ears
amidst the pain
like sentries or scouts
in the dead of night
listening to the quiet of the forest.
Deserted, the aged cock their ears
to learn more about the menace
under the stars
that are mindless
and without feeling.
They want to report –
but to whom?
Is there anyone who would do more
than pass the word on?

[1973]   (Nicholas Kolumban)

There Will Be No War

As N. N. was awaking one day at dawn, he could see the misty outline of a huge gorilla approaching his bed. Yet the creature's incredible height of more than eight feet, its six enormous fangs and a grin exceeding all human or animal proportions and with it an expression of absolute devotion to slaughter – all were so dreamlike that N. N. laid his head back on his pillow and closed his eyes with relief. His faith in the world was unshakable. The next morning – was it the following day or the following decade? – the sun found him there bleeding and torn to pieces.

[1977]   *(William Jay Smith)*

After a World Tour

In any of the few minutes left of life, I can command the sea to rush up to my feet. I do not have to step aside from the highway; it immediately provides a small boat meekly or flatteringly like the beggar extending his palm or his tin cup, the sheepdog its paw or the lady her little consenting hand. And so I journey off accordingly, standing on deck, my hair flying, a smile of voluntary exile on my face, looking forward, not backward, and humming a tune, a good old sea chantey, having emptied every glass.

With wind-swept face I have been drawn to dine with my ancestors. The question 'Where have you been today?' becomes rarer and rarer. I would like to speak of the islands and of my instructive adventures, of my distant friends and of their advice, but I could transform those remote overseas tongues into this one only with a stammer, and hence will announce only with the wave of my hand: I have been to the same place today. And I empty one final glass. Always about to depart.

[1977]   (William Jay Smith)

Before the Journey

Curled up onto themselves old men nestle in their beds
  like foetuses; and the poor body,
which in its weakness longs simply to be cradled,
  recalls how good to be once was.

And it dawns then on the body that it is not alone;
  a gentleness, rising as from its earliest home,
a warmth of almost universal power comes over it,
  mysteriously womanly.

Will this new power send, as did that other once,
  through the fluid of its arteries,
salts, calcium, hopes, genes (for an existence beyond
  this)? –
  that's what old men wonder.

And they grip their knees like paratroopers on a plane
  about to jump, and who, before they descend,
worry (though not permitted to) whether the wings on
  their back
  will open – and, if so, to what end.

[1974, published 1977]   (William Jay Smith)

This book has been published with support
from the Hungarian Ministry of Cultural Heritage
and the Frankfurt '99 Kht. (Budapest)

Co-Editor Gyula Kodolányi
Book design by Péter Horváth
Photograph by Domokos Moldován
Typesetting by Windor Bt., Budapest
Printed in Hungary by Argumentum Publishing House,
Budapest
ISBN 963 8464 90 9